Death By Shakespeare

Matt Longstaff & Chris Walker
Developed with Cait Fannin

Guided by a Bard four centuries entombed,
A troupe of merry thespians here come.
Their stage is set for a tragedy doomed,
So switch off your phones, the show has begun.
For this band of blaggards need no such props,
As joke-shop blood or retractable knives.
Their shows deliver the largest of shocks,
With death scenes so real, no actor survives.
Past care or cure these actors truly be,
Blood, bile and brains, the stage will wear them all,
And Shakespeare's terrors are performed with glee,
Until the reaper makes his curtain call.

So there's always more screaming than applause,
When the Squirmington players tread the boards.

Meet the Squirmington Players

Cleo (27)
Can't see without her glasses.
She can't find her glasses.

Director, Bill (50)
Once appeared out of focus
in a crowd scene on Eastenders,
so he's a proper thesp!

Julie (39)
In charge of tea and biscuits.

Tony (46)
Drives coaches for a living. He'd drive
the tour bus if they had one.

Claude (67)
Has been there, done that.
He doesn't talk about it though.

"Dost thou not see my baby at my breast,
That sucks the nurse asleep?"

CLEOPATRA

Cleopatra takes her life with the bite of an asp.
Act V, Scene ii - Alexandria. A room in the monument.

"A plague o' both your houses!
They have made worms' meat of me."

MERCUTIO

Tybalt stabs Mercutio.
Act III, Scene i - A public square in fair Verona.

 enRy V

"Fortune is Bardolph's foe, and frowns on him,
For he hath stolen a pax, and hanged must a' be.
A damned death!"

PISTOL

Bardolph is publicly hanged.
Act III, Scene vi - The English camp in Picardy.

Richard III

"A horse! A horse!
My kingdom for a horse!"

RICHARD III

Richard III is killed in battle after his horse is slain.
Act V, Scene vii - Bosworth Field.

" Why, there they are, both baked in this pie."

TITUS

Chiron & Demetrius are baked in a pie.
Act V, Scene iii - Court of Titus's house. A banquet set out.

"What, will these hands ne'er be clean?"

LADY MACBETH

Lady Macbeth is driven to madness.
Act V, Scene i - Dunsinane. Ante-room in the castle.

King Lear

"See't shalt thou never. Fellows, hold the chair.
Upon these eyes of thine I'll set my foot."

CORNWALL

Gloucester has his eyes plucked out and stamped on by Cornwall.
Act III, Scene vii - Gloucester's castle.

Henry VI

Part 1

> " Break thou in pieces, and consume to ashes,
> Thou foul accursed minister of hell. "

DUKE OF YORK

Joan la Pucelle is burned at the stake.
Act V, Scene vi - Camp of the York in Anjou.

> " Cut me to pieces, Volsces. Men and lads,
> Stain all your edges on me."

CORIOLANUS

Coriolanus is killed by the sword of Titus Aufidius.
Act V, Scene vi - Antium. A public place.

"O, I am slain!"

POLONIUS

Polonius is stabbed through a curtain by Hamlet.
Act III, Scene iv - The Queen's bedchamber.

Titus Andronicus

> "See, lord and father, how we have performed
> Our Roman rites. Alarbus' limbs are lopped
> And entrails feed the sacrificing fire."

LUCIUS

Alarbus has his limbs torn off and thrown into the fire.
Act I, Scene i - Rome. Before the Capitol.

 Venus and Adonis

"And, nuzzling in his flank, the loving swine
Sheathed unaware the tusk in his soft groin."

NARRATOR

Adonis is killed by a wild boar while hunting.
Line 1115-1116. The forest.

A Midsummer Night's Dream

> "Out sword, and wound
> The pap of Pyramus...
> Where heart doth hop.
> Thus die I: thus, thus, thus."

PYRAMUS

Bottom (as Pyramus) stabs himself believing his love has been eaten by a lion.
Act V, Scene i - Athens. The palace of Theseus.

" Et tu, Brute? "

CAESAR

Julius Caesar is stabbed by conspirators.
Act III, Scene i - Rome. Before the Capitol.

The inter's Tale

" Exit, pursued by a bear "

SHAKESPEARE

Antigonus is chased and eaten by a bear.
Act III, Scene iii - Bohemia. A desert country near the sea.

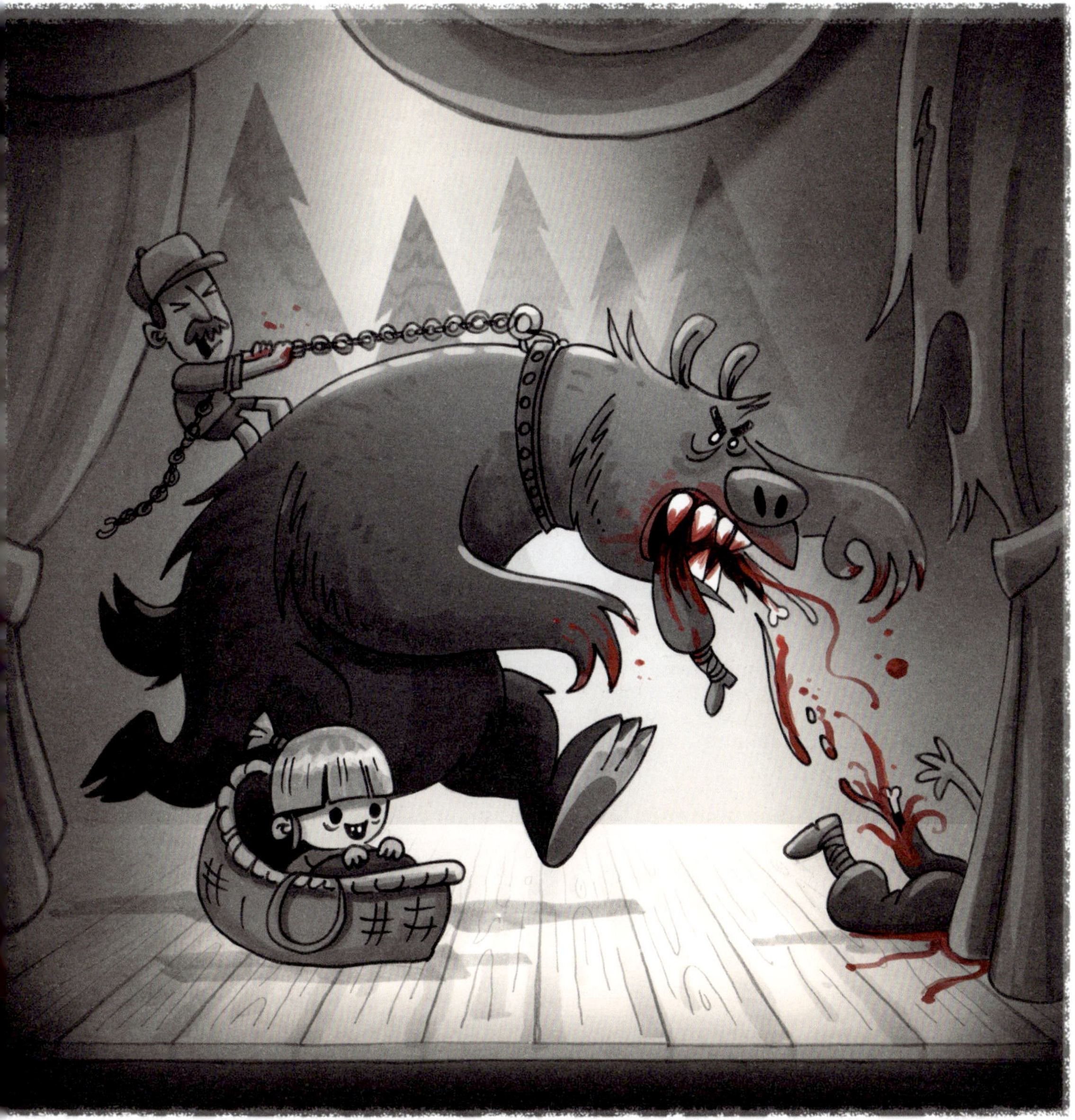

Othello

"Down, strumpet!"

OTHELLO

Desdemona is smothered with a pillow by Othello.
Act V Scene ii - A bedchamber in the castle.

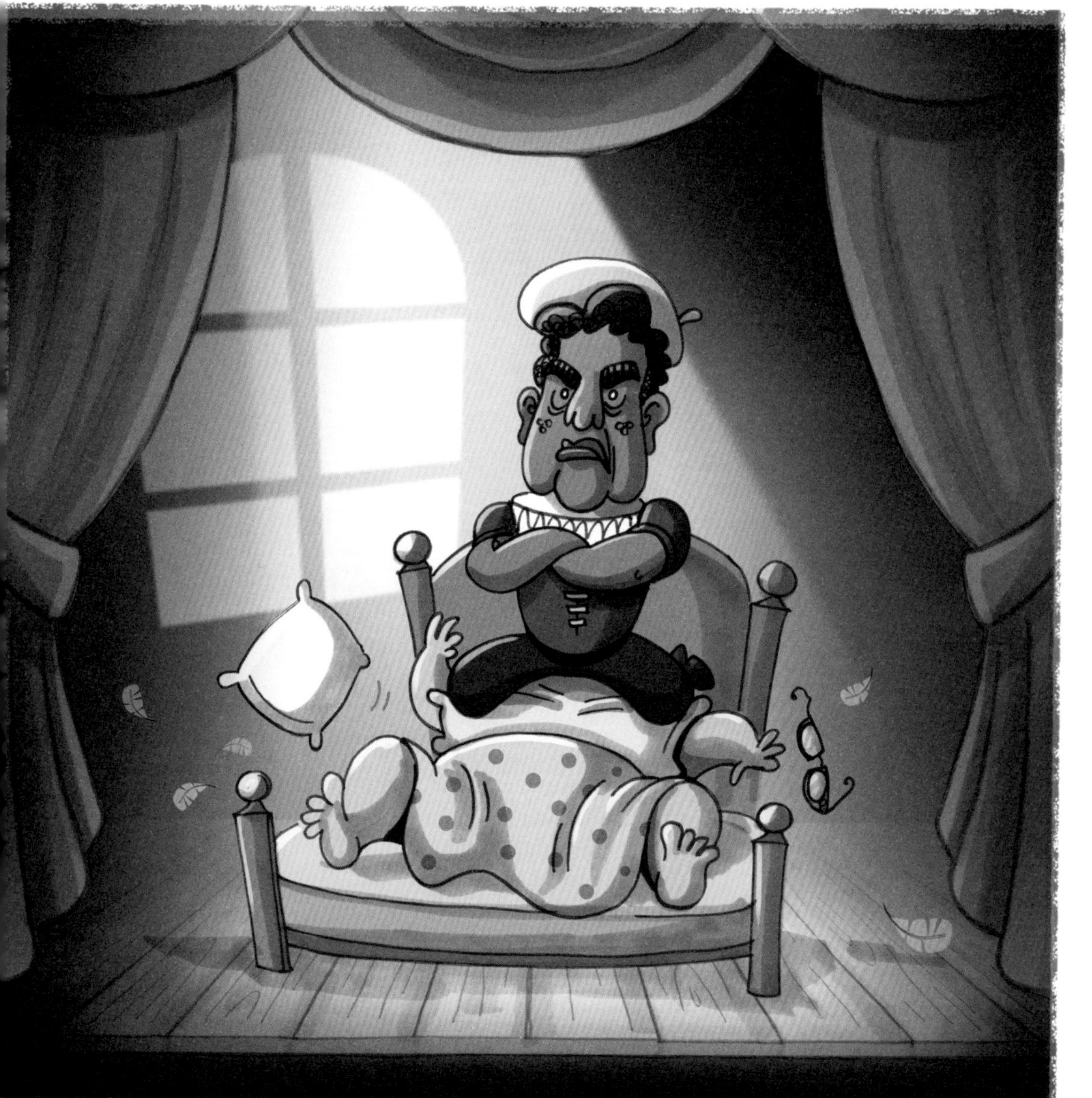

King John

"The wall is high, and yet will I leap down.
Good ground, be pitiful and hurt me not."

PRINCE ARTHUR

Trying to escape, Prince Arthur leaps from a wall and dies.
Act IV, Scene iii - Before the castle.

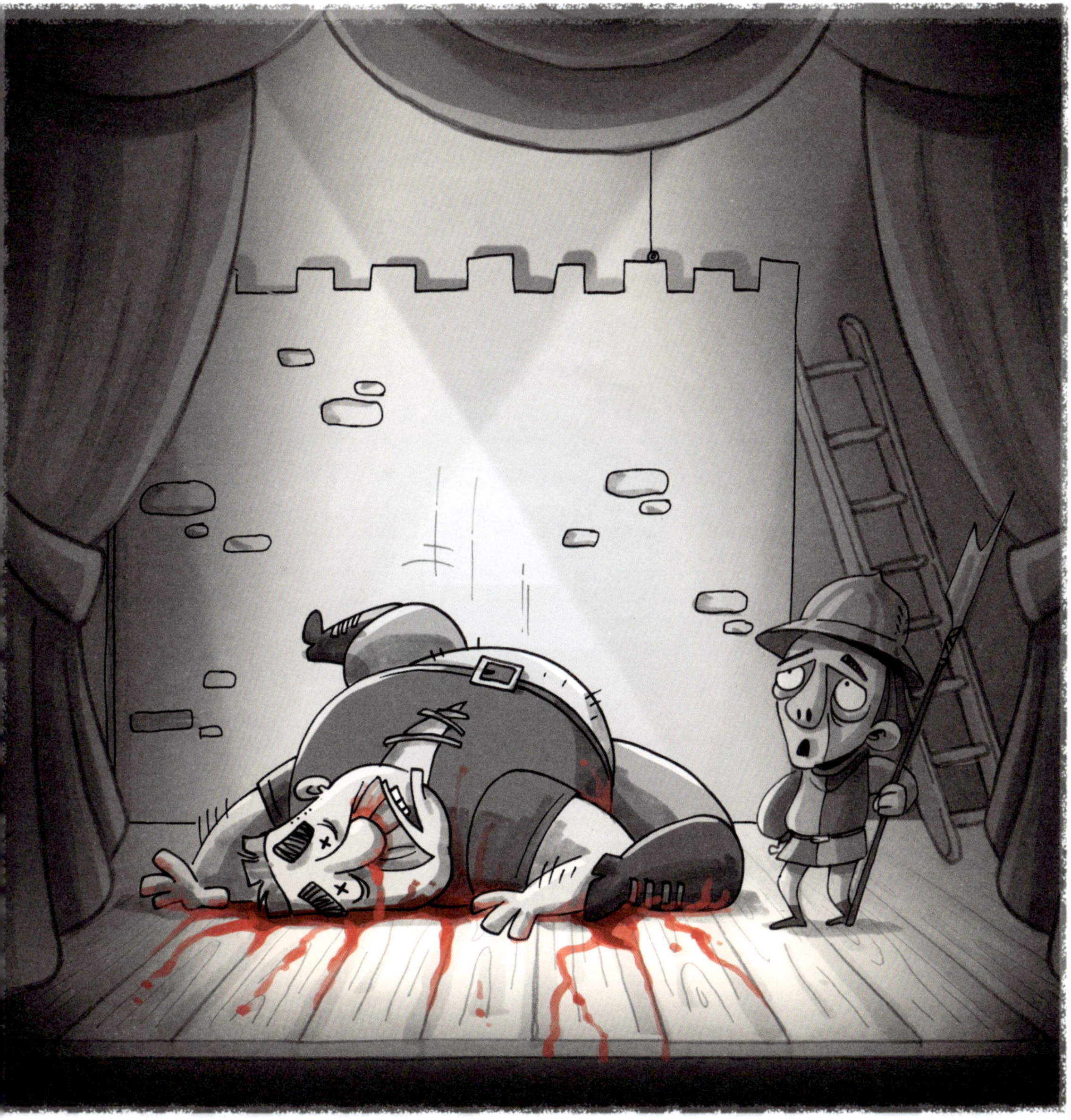

Macbeth

"I bear a charmed life, which must not yield
To one of woman born."

MACBETH

Macbeth is beheaded by Macduff.
Act V, Scene x - A Field.

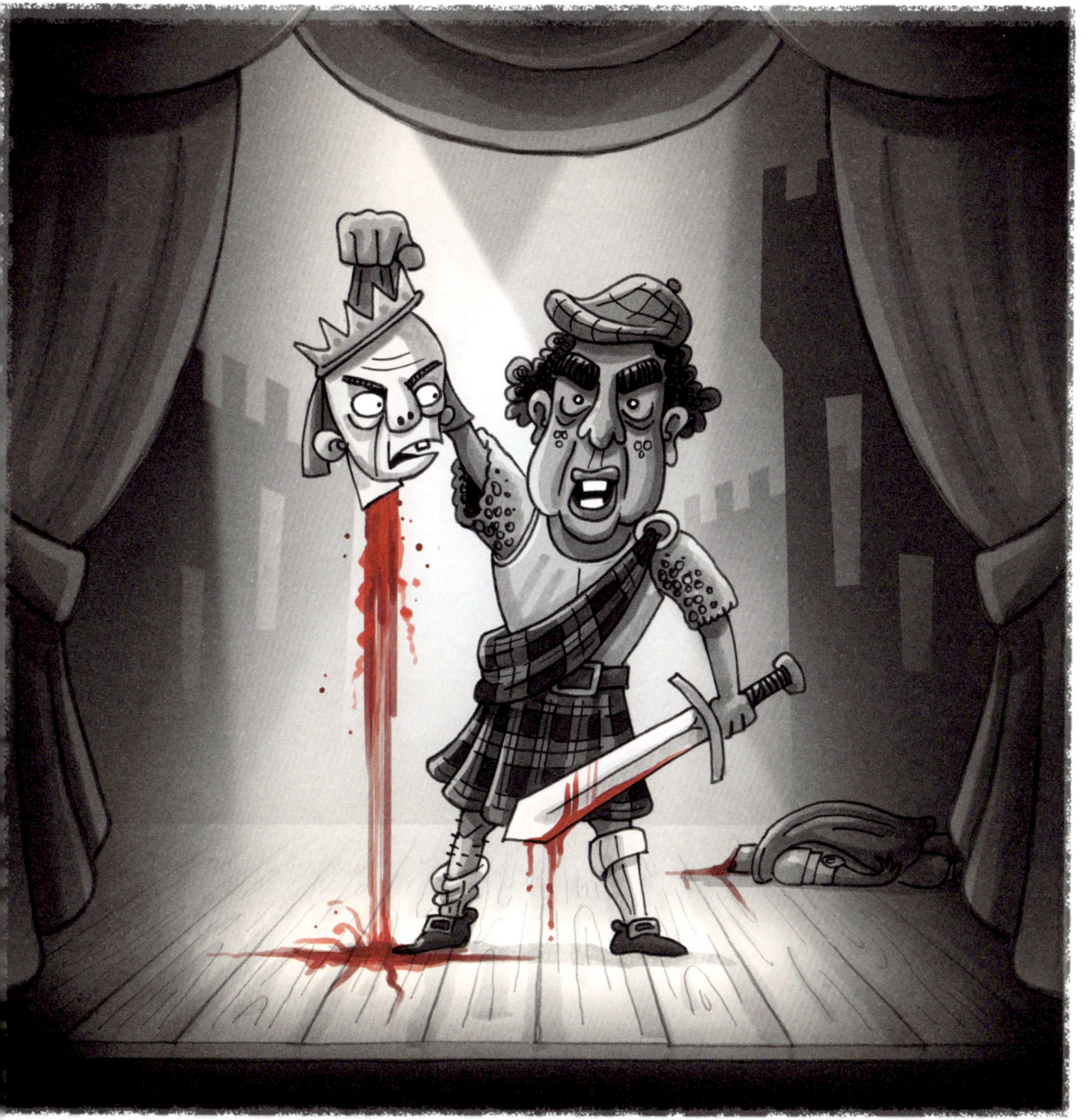

Titus Andronicus

"Set him breast-deep in earth and famish him.
There let him stand, and rave, and cry for food."

LUCIUS

Aaron is buried up to the neck and left to starve.
Act V, Scene iii - Plains near Rome.

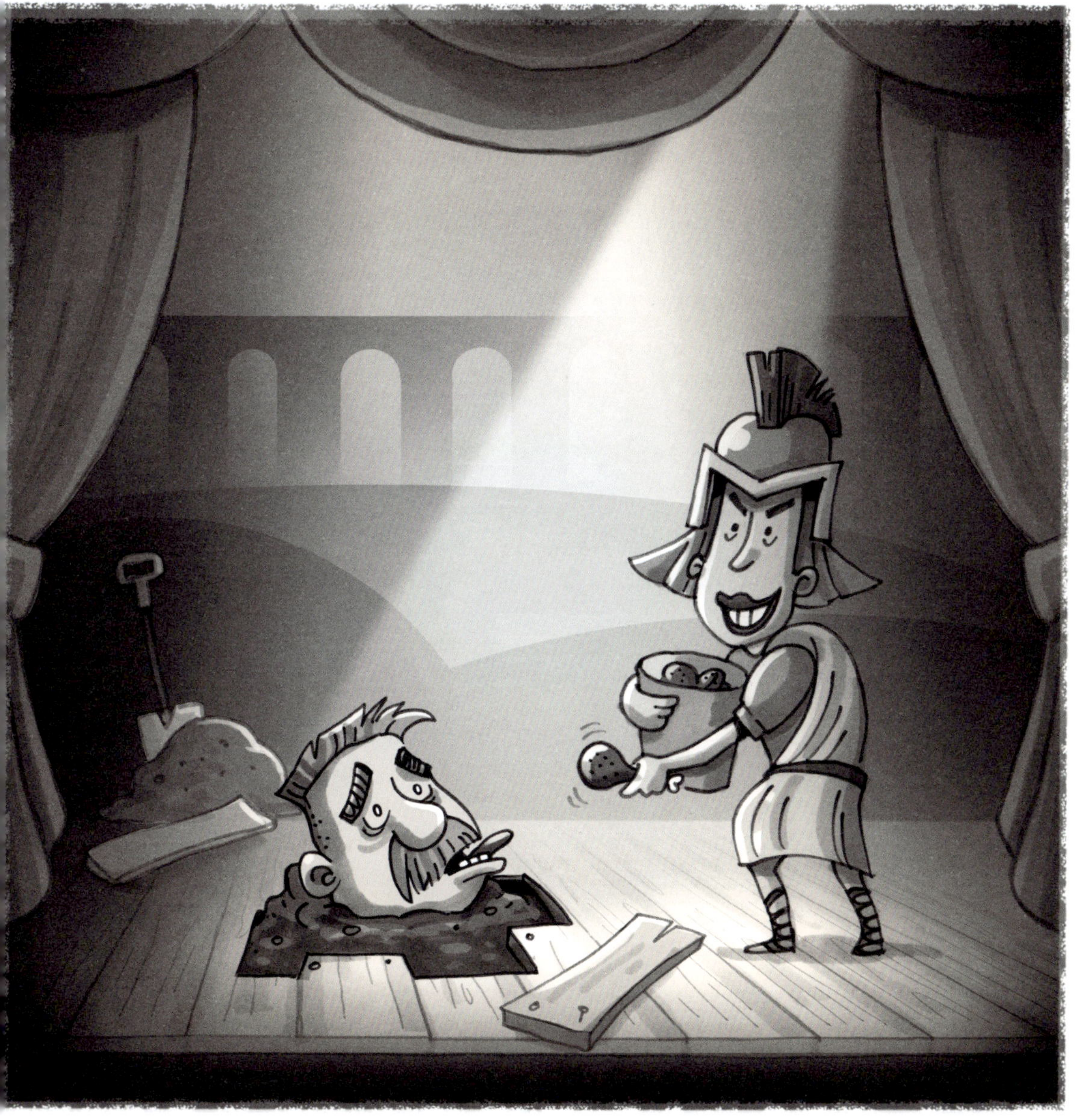

Julius Caesar

"Tear him, tear him!"

THIRD PLEBEIAN

Cinna the poet is mistaken for a conspirator and torn apart by an angry mob.
Act III, Scene iii - A street.

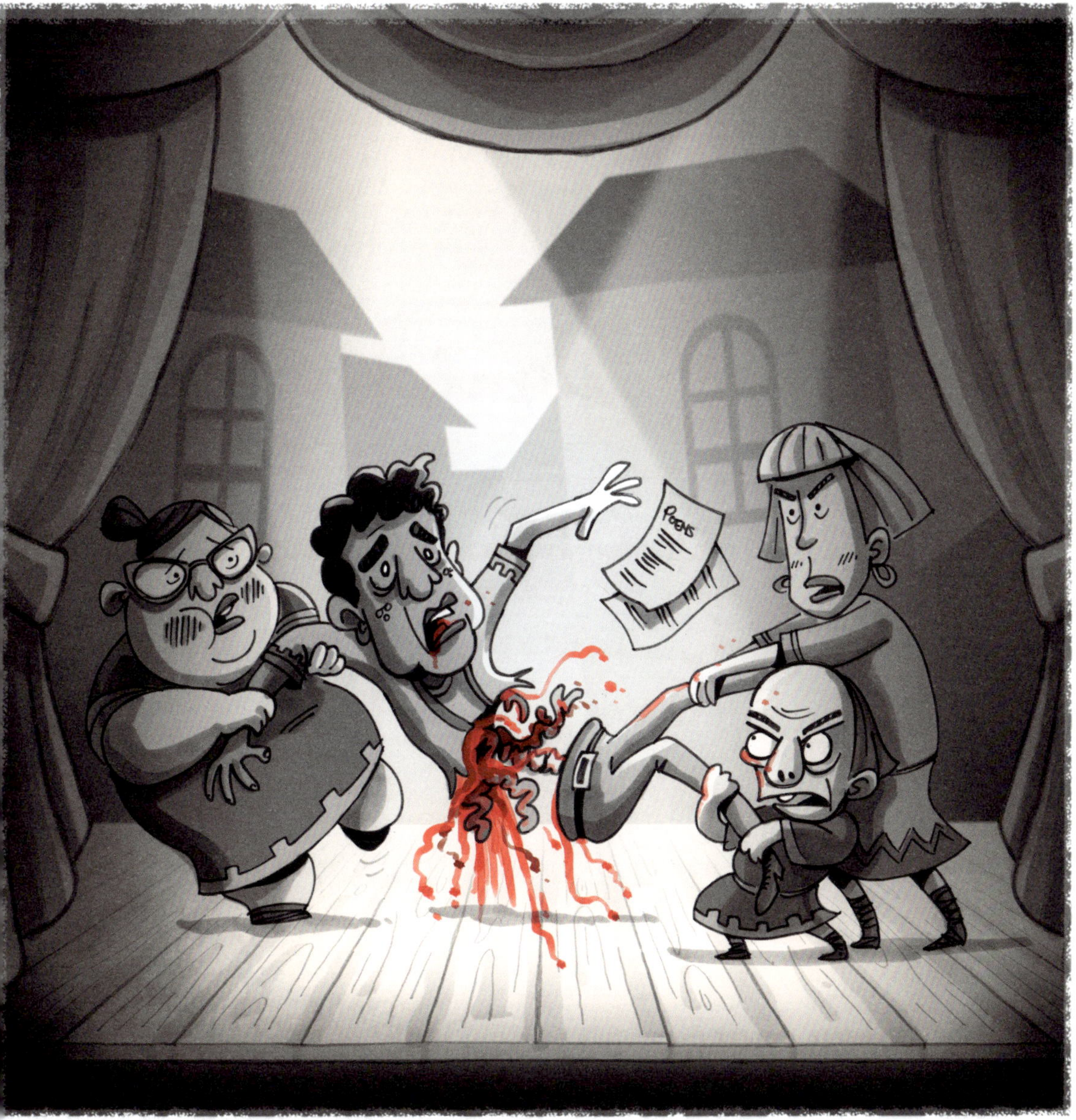
POEMS

Hamlet

"The drink, the drink! I am poisoned."

GERTRUDE

Getrude drinks poisoned wine.
Act V, Scene ii - A hall in the castle.

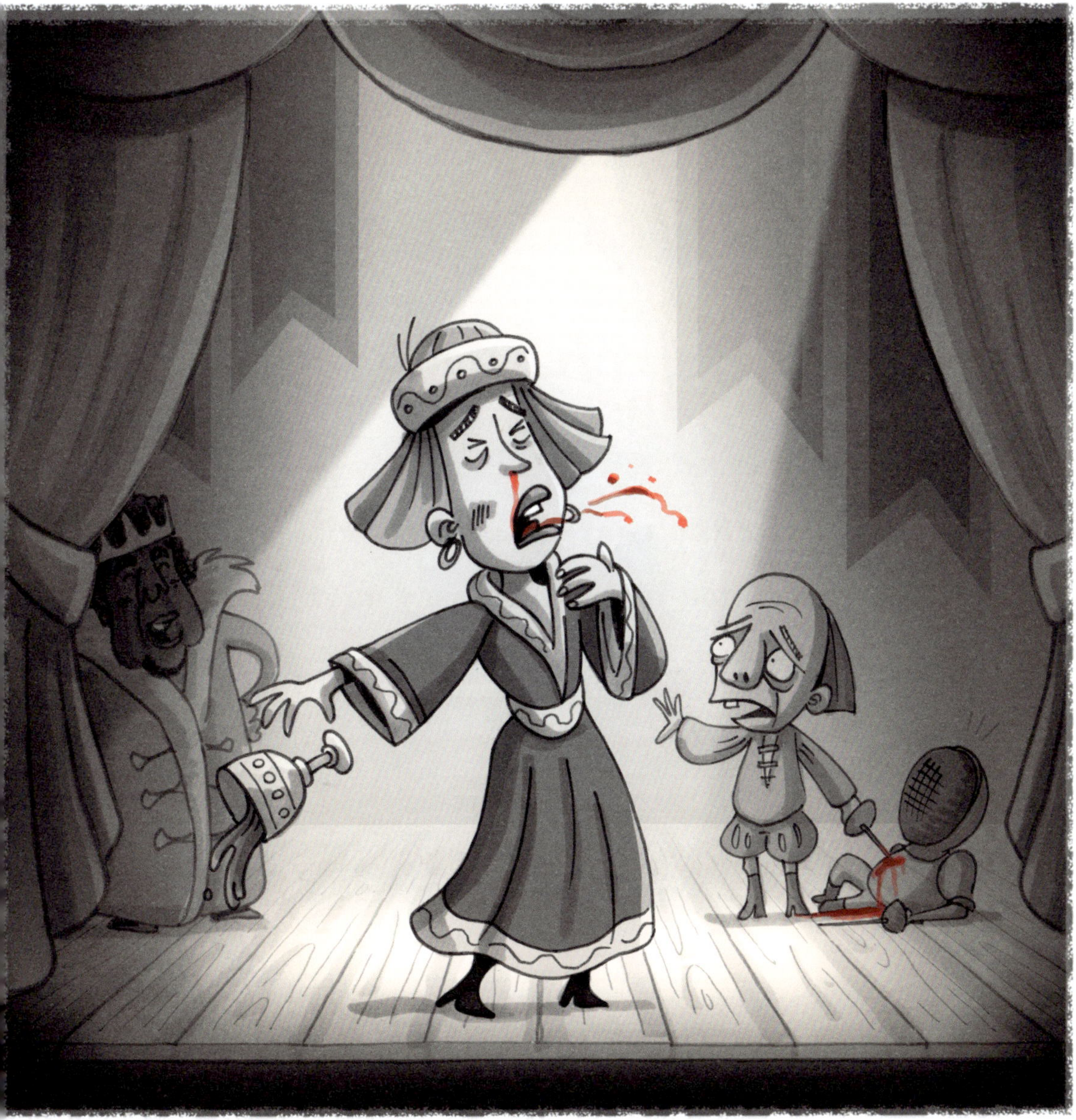

Richard III

"Take that, and that! If all this will not serve,
I'll drown you in the malmsey butt within."

FIRST MURDERER

Clarence is stabbed and drowned in a hogshead of wine.
Act I, Scene iv - London. The Tower.

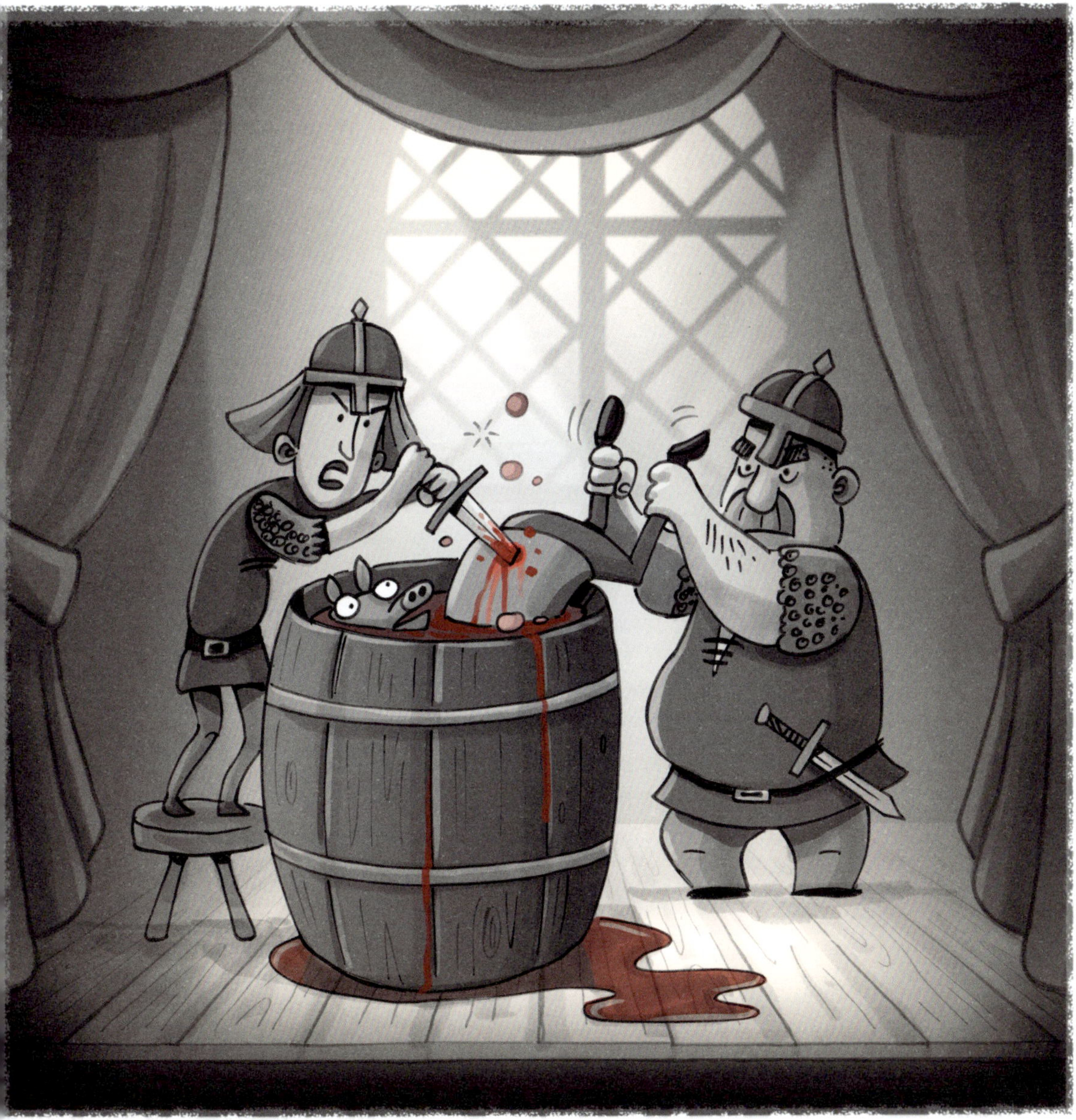

Julius Caesar

" Impatience of my absence... she fell distraught,
And, her attendants absent, swallowed fire."

BRUTUS

Portia swallows hot coals, taking her own life.
Act IV, Scene ii - Rome.

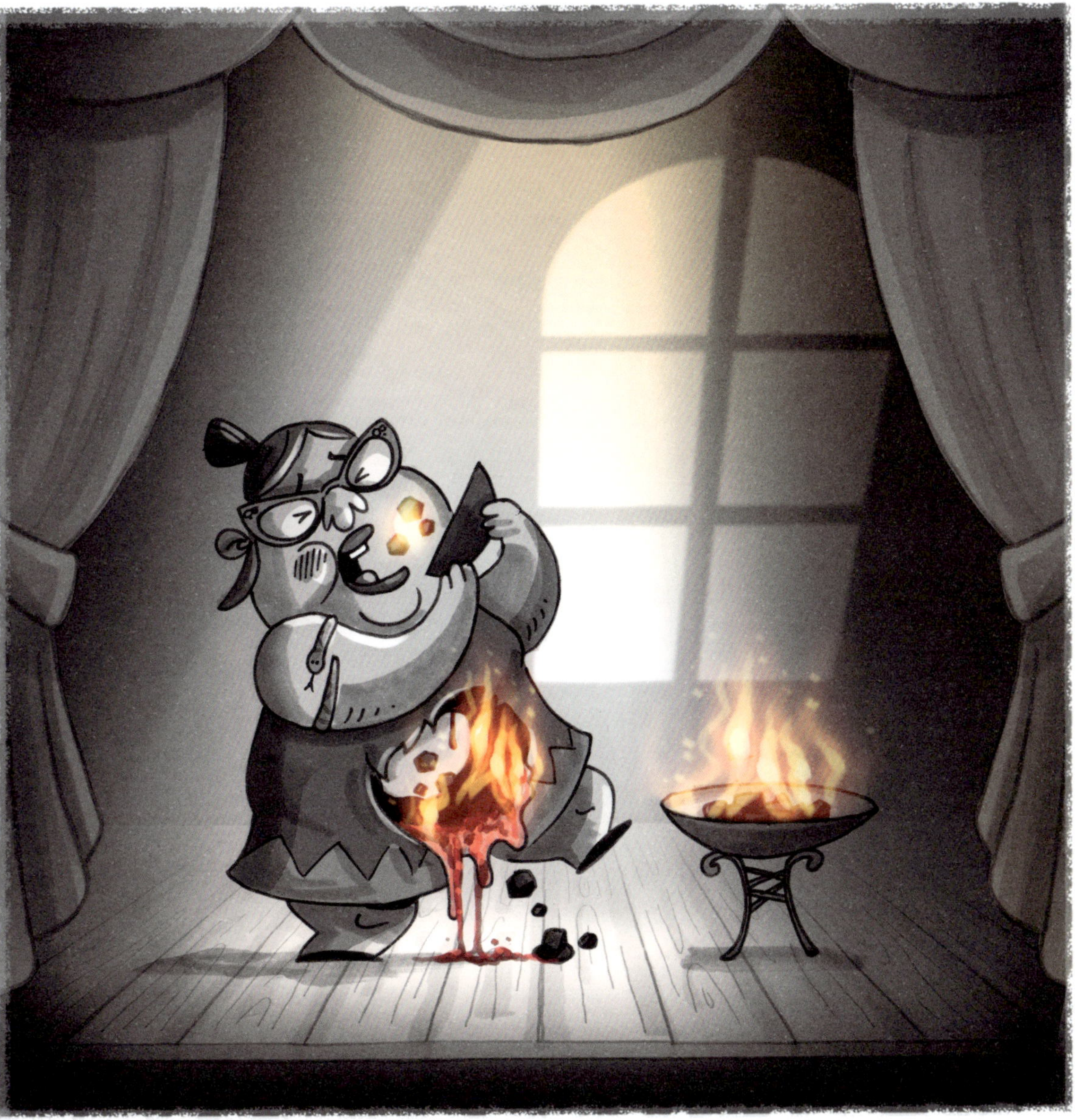

Romeo and *Juliet*

" For never was a story of more woe Than this of Juliet and her Romeo."

PRINCE

Romeo takes his life with poison, Juliet follows with his dagger.
Act V, Scene iii - Capulet tomb.

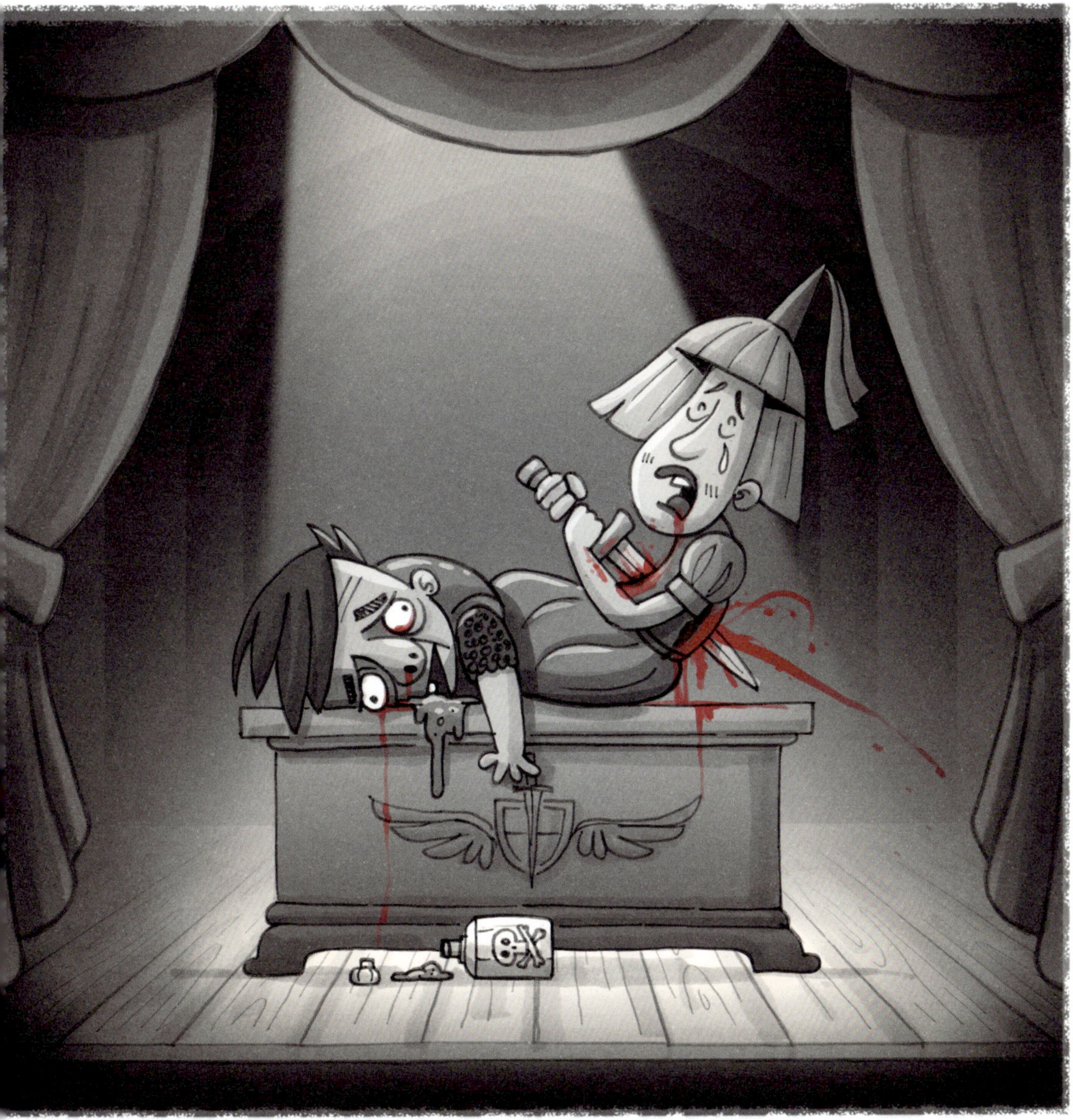

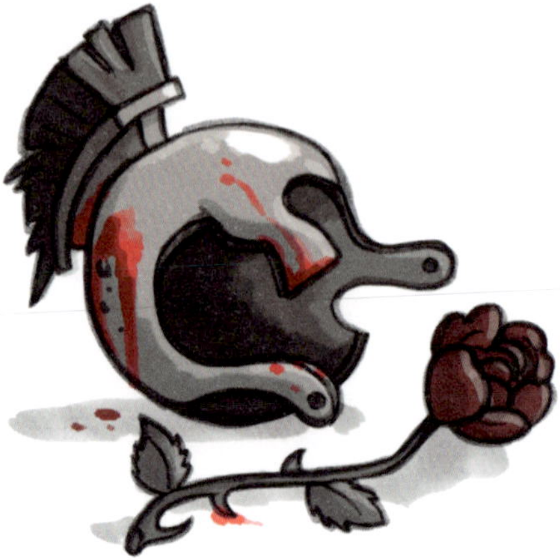

Also available from Squirm & Learn

Let's Play: MURDER

Squirm and Learn

Matt Longstaff and Chris Walker

Learn your ABC's the darkly comic way, as two troubled tearaways commit creative acts of siblicide for your learning pleasure.

Available from www.deadcanarycomics.com

THIS IS A DEAD CANARY BOOK

Copyright ©2016 by Matt Longstaff, Chris Walker & Dead Canary

Published in Great Britain in 2016 by Dead Canary Books

Dead Canary Publishing
13 Holywell Row
London
EC2A 4JF

www.deadcanarycomics.com

All illustrations by Chris Walker

All rights reserved. This book is sold on the condition that is shall not - by way of trade or otherwise - be lent, loaned or otherwise circulated without the publisher's prior written content. No part of this publication may be reproduced or transmitted in any form without explicit authorisation from the publisher.

A CIP catalogue for this book is available from the British Library

ISBN 978-0-9954572-0-1

Printed in the UK by Steve Hannah

Special thanks to: Sid, Vic, Laura,
and our favourite Kickstarter backer - Yves Jacoby

www.squirmandlearn.com
@squirm_n_learn